Human Rites

For Scottie.

Human Rites

*Great to meditate
with you
creatively*

poems
by

michael castro

Peace

Cover Photography:
Front:*Swayambhu Buddha* by Ira Cohen
Back: *Bom Shankar* by Ira Cohen
Photos of Michael Castro by Adelia Parker and Paul Neuenkirk

Cover design by Kenneth Allen

ISBN 1-931190-25-9

Neshui Publishing
45 Aberdeen
St. Louis, MO 63105
neshui62@hotmail.com

ACKNOWLEDGEMENTS

The author wishes to thank the editors of the
following magazines, anthologies, bus stop signs, and
postcard series for previously publishing poems
collected in this volume.

And What Rough Beast: Poems at the End of the Century
Auration
BigBridge (on line)
Bi-State Neighborhood Marks Project
Break Word With the World
Brilliant Corners
Bulletin of the Missouri Philological Society
Caliban Press Jazz Series
Contact II Postcard Series
The Cumberland Review
Drumvoices Revue
Edge (Japan)
First Harvest: Jewish Writing in St. Louis 1991-1997
The Forest Park Review
Focus Midwest
Grist (on line)
Half Naked Muse: Contemporary American Poetry
        (Hungary)
Ignite
Intermission
International Poetry (Brazil)
Jewish American Poetry: Poems, Commentary,
        and Reflections
Life, Liberty, and the Pursuit of Poetry
Many Moons
Memories & Memoirs: Essays, Poems, Stories, & Letters by
        Missouri Authors
The Midwest Quarterly
Miscellany (India)
Mississippi Valley Review
Nexus

Human Rites is dedicated to the poet Arthur
Brown, the photographer Morrie Camhi, and
musicians Joe Catalano, David Hines, and Maurice
Malik King. During their too-short lives, their
friendship & their art nourished my creativity.
I am grateful for their light.

CONTENTS

BIG GAME POEM

This is a poem to kill all the loneliness in America
as it is a poem to kill my loneliness too
for loneliness is an only one
a one alone & missing
something which in American is never known
& so one is alone
It is a poem to eat loneliness out of the stone
prune it out of the tree
worm it out of the fruit
weed it out of the garden
It is a poem to kill all the loneliness in the Free World
It's a poem for the highway flat as Kansas
for the rush hour traffic & the subway crush
for massage parlors & grain silos
gay bars movie stars crow caws
& 13th story corridors
It is a poem to kill all the loneliness in America
& to kill my loneliness too
(Being a Leo, I like the Grand Design)
Can't get loneliness out of my mind
America is lonely
It has a big headache
Husbands & wives cross in their lives
Lovers do not realize
  who they are
    & why they are
One
  love ceases being
    fun   & then
they are alone. . .

Leo paces the savannah. . .
There is rarely game in his range anymore
When there is, often he is not
Lonely lions (I almost said lovely) are pitiful creatures
They have lost their pride
They will cry out in pain if provoked
But this is a big game poem
It aims to kill all the loneliness in America
& my loneliness too
It goes off half-cocked, roaring—
It's aiming right at you

THE MAN WHO LOOKED INTO COLTRANE'S HORN

Me & my main man Mitch perched in the balcony
of the Village Theatre waiting for Trane & sweating
that summery May
be June of—was it '67?—I was almost
22 & anyway it was Trane's *last year*
in the flesh (if you can believe it)
the warm up act?—get this!—Ornette
& believe you me, he had blown
us away. He had this Swedish bass player, David
Izenson (a balding descendent of the harpist king),
a modest man with a beat
would always surprise you & delight with his light
touch, & when he stroked with his bow you wanted to bow
before the otherworldly beauty, the fertile soundshape,
you wanted to bury your head in the cave
of that Venus of Venusdorf resonating to his biblical embrace.
Right then I began a life-long love affair
with the fat fat fiddle & we wondered
how anyone could follow such a set
had set the stage, warmed us up to fever fervor,
tuned our sensory apparatus to frequencies so fine
you could see
ghosts of the Yiddish Theatre this dusty cavern used to be
floating by the drab curtain—Menasha Skulnick, dapper, bobbing
to the *b-b-b-bum b-b-b-bum* beat, the snake charming wail
of klezmer cafe reverie, & Molly Goldberg leaning out the window
of *yenta* heaven, shifting her spotlit palm from *oy vey*! mouth
to lotus ear, to forehead, shading sax-squinting eyes
as if peering down the tunnel of some lost subway station of the cross-
eyed homeless goddess, searching for the Trane who now was
officially late—late as only a ghost can know—no one
produced Yiddish plays anymore, the language was dying,
but the jazz of language,
the funny language of jazz still lived
at the Village Theatre & the Trane that we all came to catch,
& be borne away by, Trane was overdue.

Though the air had been conditioned to a degree,
it had not been cooled.
We were hot & damp in the dusty seats, drifting, leaning
back to where we were—New York, the Lower East Side,
the Sixties—The mean streets leaned in, hairy with hippies,
skittish with speed freaks, pulsing with poor Puerto Ricans—
        only the Village Theatre & the well-fed
cockroaches remained from storied days of threadbare
immigrant memories. Trane would come. Trane would take us away.
But who knew Trane himself
was dying? O sure, the sun,
Ra, was dying too. In time. But more
immediately. . .
Dying was Vietnam. Vietnam's
death consciousness
was everywhere.
Vietnam had our numbers & Mitch & I were going
anywhere but there—Canada, jail,
certifiably nuts—1-Y, 4-F. CO, AWOL whatever
it took to avoid that cold drafty death-trip.
JFK was long gone. LBJ had saddled up
the fat bullet bombs.
Bobby, Martin, Malcom—their days were numbered too.
But Trane? Trane was like Bird. I mean
his notes were scribed in the air. In the cosmos. & now
we sensed he was in the hall. You could hear the shuffling
backstage. & suddenly, without fanfare, the curtain sidled open.

Dark forms crowded the shrouded stage.
We could make out Alice, stomping
chords on the baby grand, & that must've been Jimmy
Garrison plucky at the bass,
& they were flanked by an assemblage
of street-wise percussionists – congas, bongos, traps, gongs,
talking drums, bell-trees, mbiras, dombeks, vibes – all emoting
a kind of cacophonous swelling, a biomorphic mass
vibrating something like thunder & bird thought shifting
to the sound they say a tornado makes up close

4

swirling over the hillside. The ensemble
built a kind of primordial chaos, something
from the nothingness they shared, that shared them,
taking away our breath, & restoring us
to a breathless awareness, an alert anticipation
of an electrical storm of violent renewal—

& then Trane emerged from the wings like a god
blowing in full stride & he reached out
with a finger of sound to the assembled host charging
the eye of their hurricanish brew with a gleam of life's coherent
insistent yearning, & they & we were off,
flying—Trane was down to earth,
business-like in an unremarkable brown suit. His face was
serious & intense & he was blowing something beyond
harmony & rhythm, melodic snatches from riverbanks of memory,
from the silt of the soul, interspersed between cries,
moans & laughs, & another music that was as if
he had wired his brain for sound & was playing the 90%
we supposedly don't use, levels of consciousness finding form
& expression in the awesome moment, the world's
madnesses & wars
swallowed in his inspired breath
& spit out with all their raw & jagged edges
painful & explosive & expansive—
horribly beautiful in the larger patterns.
There was a point—how far into the set I couldn't say—
for after the initial shamanic shock we were with him,
beyond musical or chronological time—
but a point in this newly created space was reached
when something strange
went down. A man rose from his aisle seat like an island
rising from the sea, a long lanky baldheaded, blue
peacoated black man rose, & as if drawn by an invisible life-line
bounded over the sound waves & leapt onto the floating stage
to stand & shimmer & smile mesmerically close
to the saxophonic source.
Trane took no notice, immersed in his immense immanence,

& the man smilingly swayed as Coltrane played. . . *a few of my*
favorite things. . . booo-waah! eeyaah! . .
      as Trane took us out
to those unchartered places once again the man shook
electrically registering each shock
wave & then turned
& peered down into the depths
of Trane's horn for forever it seemed
& then he looked back out to the oceanic
audience beatific & believing like Big Foot
must have appeared after he stared into the hat of the Ghost
Dance prophet & saw in that emptiness
the whole world—

Trane kept playing & the man stayed up there swaying
& then suddenly Trane stopped, nodded to Alice & let her lead
the percussive swells of the underlying soundsea, & he turned
& threw his arm around the silent witness, & walked him toward
the wings, whispering god
knows what
in his ear. The man
clambered down the sidestage steps & back to his seat on the aisle
& within moments Trane re-emerged to make us gasp at his rumbling
train of thought, & then again the man bounded & leaped aboard
& swayed & grimaced & smiled & buried his head deep
into the golden Selmer flume so that we could see the light
of spot gleaming off his bald brown dome as Trane played
implacably unperturbed through the intrusion, literally played
through the head
of the magnetized initiate—undampened, unwound
galactic, genetic spirals of philosophic sound – played
from some invisible mountaintop
through all our heads the unfamiliar familiar epic notes,
mapped journeys through this world & others
& brought us all home to

A Love Supreme
A Love Supreme
A Love Supreme

    *

eventually
       the man left the stage
       shaking his ringing head,
eventually
       we all left the theatre
       to journey our own
       seedy East Village streets,
eventually
       even the ghosts left
       the Village Theatre
       to its incarnation as the Fillmore East rock
       palace, & suddenly

Trane left the set,
left this plane & planet
whose pain & madness & beauty
       he'd exposed
to his *obeah* belly & breath—
having spit his medicinal music on us
through his healing horn & falseface lips,
       Trane left us one night
insights, lessons, sounds
ringing his bottomless bell through all our heads,
like a blue locomotive Trane left us
& kept on playing

through, beyond

all the wars
& all the love
in eternity
within us all

NAGASWARUM PLAYERS IN ALL SAINTS CHURCH
W/ OLIVER LAKE

The sound converges from all four sides of the vast room—
unearthly, earthy, raucus, jagged, round—
four Nagaswarum players
in walking talking meditation,
gravitating toward a living center.
Alan Suits brought these long black hardwood horns back with him
from India along with a supply of reeds; he blows
from the East, Jay Zelenka blows from the West,
Jim Marshall blows from the North, & I blow from the South.
It's the Universe City
Nagaswarum Orchestra. No one is ready for this—
not here in the 1973 Midwest. But we're ready, heady with the
                  overlapping drones, hearing
& feeling the music vibrate head to toe, filling the space
we inhabit—All Saints Church—Father Kelly
lets us practice here Wednesday nights when no one's around,
                  thinks we're a rock band
he's keeping off the streets. O the soundscape we create!
Nagaswarum,
ancient gatekeeper's horns, inside the palace now, threatening
to tumble the walls. Interior Gabriels. We rock
all right & night. Solid
ancient rock consciousness.
Massive movement of sound, inevitable as lava flow.
Rick Safron tinkles little bells
like water spraying above our seascape.

The saxophonic wind wails in the front door, billowing
with it sweet scents of gigantic flowers, herb teas & pollen.
Our noses wiggle,
ears perk. We are refreshed inside our breaths. Oliver Lake
has found his way to this suddenly sacred
rec-room of All Saints.
His saxophone harmonizes, melodizes

8

with these nasty nagaswarum.
The intelligent sound smiles,
having found its long lost relatives.
The Universe City night is intimate as eternity.
We instinctively reconfigure as petals round Lake's flower,
as solar system, as karmic wheel of life. We understand
whale song inside & out.
Lake's monkish bald spot shines
in the center of our shrinking expanding circle.
All the saints look down, smiling.
Father Kelly turns over somewhere in his bed.
Strange forms invade his dreams.
Outside, autumn leaves fall & skitter along gray city streets.

No one is ready for this music.

the pronoun "it" = life

IF YA WANNA RIDE IT
GOTTA RIDE IT LIKE YA FIND IT

Trust the flow Joe
you never know
just where you'll go
but you get there o-
k—here today
as they *say*
what?

*trust where life
will take you
despite obstacles or
changed events; you'll
get through life okay*

Trust the flow Joe
the juice'll rush
the river gush
& pause because
it must—
The laws
the laws are in-
eluctable—
the shadow
cannot be held
o no

*life's passions +
the times of quiet
are essential
universal laws
not to be avoided — inevitable*

*shadows have no substance
(also considered the negatives)*

Trust the flow Joe
just try & meld
yourself into the fabric
of the whole—
not to say
in any way
the soul—
but just the blend
of tree & roots & earth
or
on another plane
the simultaneous birth
of breath
& death
remains

*learn to value all
life — to attain a
Oneness w/ all in
the cosmos*

*life + death part of
the cycles*

10

unexplained

Trust the flow Joe
whatever you did is done
whatever you had is gone
you'll never find
what's left behind
yet today's new sun
is the same old one
& the waves you've begun
keep moving on

Trust the flow Joe

*don't dwell on the
past — it's gone*

*life is a continued
flow — one we are part
of — know its universal
laws & go w/ it*

BLEW IT
for Woody Shaw

through the tobacco haze
& the clatter of cocktails
through the stench of spilled beer
& the lurching boilermakers
out of the darkness of the pit
where the vipers of the night entwine
he gave language to the black rose

Yeah, they said, he gave language
to the emptiness they shared
he gave them prayer & they said, *Yeah*

he screeched from the ache in his balls
intricate & instinctive as a spider
his belly blown lines spun a symmetry
spanning the void, flies buzzed quizzically
round his notes on their way to the silent gods
& the chorus echoed *Yeah*
as he quenched their summer thirst

He was troubled, he was troubled
by their trouble, for he took it on
sucked it into the bell of his horn
into his gut where it gnawed & got reborn
made it part of his own storm
& he rained, he rained like a dark cloud
he reigned regal as a pharoah, clean as a queen
o he fluttered like a monarch, like Chuang Tzu,
like a caterpillar waking up & finding out
he can fly

& no one wondered why, they just let him die
they just said, *Yeah,* & let him die

for he gave language to the black rose
& down, down in the dankness where its root grows
the cyclopean train shrieked in the tunnel of the soul
a thousand toilets flushed & the excrement of the city rushed
& gargled through the labyrinthine network of subway pipes
a murderous *shakti* current injected the third rail eye
with a lobotomous blindness he straddled—
sinking his feet in the low slow quicksand—
They said *Yeah*, & lashed him to the tracks
O he had to hear that iron Siren's song

When it came hurtling & wailing out of the darkness
he had to sing along
had to embrace that Golgothan face
for it was late & he was headed home
He'd had too much to drink & he couldn't think
He just blew what he knew to be true
giving language to the black rose
raining all over it so it grows

& no one wondered why
they just said *Yeah*, & let him fly

ST. LOUIS BLUES REVISITED

Blue is the blues of this town
& blue are the bars that burn
the night down like a candle
Blue is the blues of this town

Blue is the blues of this town
Blue heat street sign blue core flame
Gas blue blaze haze glazes a name
Blue is the blues of this town

Blue is the rain song that hums & comes
From blue whale clouds that rumble like drums
Blue is the blues of this town
Blue is the blues of this town

Blue is the whiskey that gnaws in the gut
Blue is the uniform makes a man strut
Blue is the lead in the gun chamber rut
Blue is the blues of this town

Blue is the ghetto, blue the stone rubble
Blue the dope powder, blue the hope bubble
Blue are the trains, the veins, the migraines
Blue is the blues of this town

Blue is the ballpark, blue all the museums
Blue the caged monkey who swings between screams
Blue is the Arch, & the gateway of dreams
Blue is the blues of this town

Blue is the hit-man, blue in a bottle
Blue is the street girl, blue her eye shadow
Blue is the beat of the street & the news
Blue is the blues of this town

Blue is the song, blue the bird songster
Language as long & as strong as a dinosaur
The trees' teeth are chattering—airplane chainsaw
Blue is the blues of this town

Blue is the smoke over rims of the stacks
Blue is the waterfront, blue both sides of tracks
Blue is the love that is eaten by cracks
Blue is the blues of this town

AXEMAN IN THE WOODS IN WINTER
for Julius Hemphill

He swung his saxophone in the streets
& begged in red longjohns
He swung for his shadow on the wall
          for a mound of white powder
          for a dollar bill rolled in his nose
He swung up & down the street in his red longjohns
People looked some listened all moved on
He swung his axe in the dense subway
He swung it down by the riverbank
He swung it across the Brooklyn Bridge
He swung for the clouds for the herds of horses they became
          for sad folks down in their cups
          for the little boy who listened
He swung in his red longjohns
He thot of swinging with a monkey & a cup
          but didn't want no monkey on his back
He thot of swinging for the President
          but didn't want to lay down that track
He swung his own thots & didn't want
He swung for truth, for pain, for the action
          in abstraction
He swung for the pure clear ring he imagined
He swung to shake the bones round in their fleshbag
          to hear them grind together, to cast them out
          like dice
He swung because it was something he did
Maybe he swung because nobody cared
He swung to feel himself, to find himself
          to heal himself, unwind himself
He swung every day under the sun
Because it was cold outside
          he wore red longjohns

CHUMP CHANGE
for David Hines

Nick hunches into Europa Bar.
His sportcoat is shiny with soil
& his face's deep wrinkles match the coat's
dark creases. Once
well-known as a saxophone player
whose night beat covered this jazz & river city
tucking it in with flowing, anguished, shimmering sheets;
in recent years we'd seen him rarely, & then only as
a ghost of his former self, hungry & roaming
the crumbling streets, spaced out & filthy—
wrinkles like river-ruts
cut by a flood of electro-shock)))(((waves
scarring his beachy face, leaving it
a worn shell, a burnt-out case. Rumors
of drug problems, money problems, love
problems, a crack-up, breakdown, Bliss
(the mental ward), the work-house, swirled round his name
like thin smoke of a smoldering butt.

Nick drags himself into Europa & focuses
on our cheery foursome, bubbling & laughing
beneath the blank TV; & in our midst he recognizes
cherubic David, a former musical chum
& now well-known as the mellowest trumpeter in town.
Nick arches his St, Louis self, strides right up
& for openers, blows:

> "Haven't eaten in two days. . .
> Been sleeping in this sorry suit. . .
> Spent last night in City Jail. . .
> Got released this morning. Guess what? . .
> Crossed Market Street & found this. . .
> I should say this found me. . ."

He flashes from his inside pocket
a paperback book. It's a copy of *Vincent Van Gogh's
Journals,* with one of Van Gogh's haunted self-portraits
printed in blazing red on the cover.
We look up from the image of those flames
to Nick's sad, sallow mug.

He looks David in the eye:
    "Can you lend me ten dollars, Dave?
    I'll pay you back next month."

David screws up his soft round face.
It's just dawning on him who this is before him,
supplicating in the silence.
"Nick," he muses. "Now wait a quick
minute, Nick. . . How

you gonna be able to meet such a heavy
commitment,
                Nick,
seeing as we only see each other now
once every ten or fifteen years?"

Nick comes back,
        building, developing his theme:
    "Give me five dollars, man.
    If I don't pay you back. . .
    I'll give you my horn."

David winces, bows, shakes his head, smiles: "No,
don't give me your horn, brother."

    "Can you lend me three dollars," Nick wheedles,
    his voice rising. "Three dollars!
    Come on David, man. We used to jam
    together!"

David, trying to lighten the sound,
& playing to an audience, sighs,
"You drive a hard bargain, Nick."

Nick returns on time to the head:
    "Come on, man. I haven't eaten."

David digs
  into his pocket, gathers
 a palmful of silver, says,
"OK, I'll give you some change.
Get you a bowl of soup or something."

Nick accepts the coins, caresses
them without expression.
Shifts their weight in his palm.
    "Chump change. . ." he murmurs,
    softly, flatly.

David double takes, elaborates:
"Don't know
whether it's chump change or not,
but it'll get you something to eat."

Nick turns offstage, slipping
to some unheard beat toward the door.
Suddenly he whirls & shouts:
        "YOU GOT ANY MORE MONEY!"
climaxing his thematic erection.

David, softly, steadfastly:
"Got no more money
 to give away. . ."

They stare at one another,
locked in a long, sad, silent note.

Nick gathers himself again,
& says good-bye,
shaking his head &
naming each one of us
with incredible care & precision,
lingering, enunciating syllables:

    "Good-bye Dreadhead. . .
    "Good-bye Beard. . .
    "Good-bye Short-stuff. . .
    "Good-bye Axe-man. . .
    "Good-bye. . . Good-bye. . ."
        & fades. . .

David, ruefully:
"Bye, Nick.
Don't give away your horn now
for five dollars."

BECOMING KRISHNA

Gopalakrishnan, the South Indian flutist, offstage
is unimpressive—slight,& frail-looking
in the men's room mirror,
with ashy shoulder length hair a-scraggle, sunken eyes,
a hang-dog look—but
on stage, he transforms,
swells with power, inflated by the music
he pours himself into,
seated on rug'd floor, drawing up something
from beyond breath's bottom.

Gopalakrishnan: becoming
Krishna, Vishnu incarnate: god,
friend, lover,
cowherd, toddler,
never missing a beat
in the rhythms of time & condition,
the creative force,
maintainer, sustainer—

Goplakrishnan:
attentive to the grinning mrdangumist
cradling his barrel drum, vibrationally
nurturing the blind violinist, giving them
all the play they need, pouring them tea
during blowing breaks,
touching them with eyes, hands, coaxing three plus
hours of ever expanding music,
lotus petals unfolding endlessly,
transforming each
before our own transforming
ii's.

"A musical architecture of precise forms—"
classical ratios, golden means
to ends beyond
words & images—
                    the blind man
led, feebly tottering, to his place,
aglow with vision, the buck-toothed
drummer with the not-quite-all-there look:
on another plane

one sees all in the timeless heavens,
the other takes the measure of the ticking earth;

& Gopalakrishnan binds them in harmony,
breathes life
through his flute,
smiling at each, & us—

something else at play as well

NURTURE/NATURE

offering
what is needed

a little water
a sunny smile
a touch
a caring word

nurturing

we are
most human
most humble
most god-like

FREEDOM RING
for Dr. Martin Luther King

Dr. King, Dr. King,
When did you hear freedom ring?

When the bloodhounds growled & wailed?
When sheriffs locked you up in jail?
When you sat up front in a bus?
When you overcame for us?

Dr. King, Dr. King,
When did you hear freedom ring?

When the tap clicked on your phone?
When you prayed at night alone?
When a child returned your smile?
When you walked the extra mile?

Dr. King, Dr. King,
When did you hear freedom ring?

With civil rights writ into law?
With klansmen pounding at the door?
When you won the Nobel Prize?
When you looked into deep dark eyes?

Dr. King, Dr. King,
When did you hear freeedom ring?

When you lunched with congressmen?
When you marched with garbagemen?
When your dream lit up the night?
When your soul beamed in the light?

Dr. King, Dr. King,
When did you hear freedom ring?

When you climbed the mountain high?
When the bullet let you die?
When your spirit rose to speak?
When you turned the other cheek?

Dr. King, Dr. King,
When did you hear freedom ring?

MA

When I came to you
I was but a seed
woven out of mystery
fashioned out of need
You fed me with your body
& you fed me with your mind
You were always there for me
You were always kind

 & no one
 but you
 would do
  & I knew

When I came to you
Everything was dark
You opened up my eyes
& you showed me how to walk
You showered me with kisses
& you bathed me with your tears
You ran your hands all over me
& washed away my fears

 & no one
 but you
 would do
  & I knew

When I came to you
I had never seen the light
I had only known the darkness
I had only known the night
You smiled the changing moon & stars
Then lifted up the sun
You showed me multiplicity
& then you showed me One

    & no one
    but you
    would do
       & I knew

When I came to you
You opened up your door
You gave me all your riches
& you offered me more
You gave me a map
& you gave me a key
You held me so close to you
& then you set me free

    & no one
    but you
    would do
       & I knew

SNAPSHOT OF AN INFANT,
WINKING

old man
    baby

  looking out
      looking in

DEEP MIRROR
for Katherine Dunham

She digs an endless root, cuts, transplants
Sets herself up as a root doctor in a powerful swamp
Sets herself up all right, sets herself all upright
She digs an endless root this doc of dance

Holds a mirror up to each patient's breath she do
Holds a sea up to a setting sun *o yeah*
Walks that same path Damballa Wedo do each day o
Slides across the sky on that endless root *hey*

Root doctor dancing, the root twists & turns
Flames leap at the center, the heart weeps & yearns
A flaming swamp flower reaches up to the sky
& down into the earth where the living must die

She digs an endless root, cuts, transplants
In the powerful swamp where the two rivers meet
The cuttings take hold through the earth, of the dance
Of the blue people waking & quaking their feet

Gatekeeper Legba, an old man in tatters
leans on his crutch in the dust of the path
He points with his pipe & its tiny fire
to a place you can't see but know matters

Root doctor dancing, the flames dancing too
The garden is growing where the people are blue
She holds up a mirror that's deep as a gun
She offers an ocean to a serpentine sun

Ghede sits dapper at the edge of a circle
His cigarette dangles, right leg's crossed over knee;
Behind his shades an underworld darkens
Look in his eye dancer, whose "i" do you see?

She digs an endless root, cuts, transplants
The dead are awakened by the din of the dance
Root doctor swaying, the *loa* arise
They shine in her eyes now, she seems in a trance

Erzulie is mounting a bucking *bon ange*
She rides now in terror, she rides now in grace
She rides over the sea to the mouth of the river
She leaves you behind & she smiles through your face

Doc digs an endless root, cuts through & transplants
Sea flows through the rivers & sings in the swamps
Blue people buckle, Damballah still shines
& Shango speaks surely through the cracks in time

Root Doctor the patient, the patient revive
Root Doctor I didn't think that patient alive
The mirror is cloudy, spirit floats in a mist
The sun's in its bed now, the sea has been kissed

Root doctor *loa*, root doctor up right
Root doctor darkness & root doctor light
Endless root opens the gate of the night
Serpent sun memory speckled & bright

Holds a mirror up to each patient's breath she do
Holds a sea up to a setting sun *o yeah*
Walks the same path Damballah-Wedo do we do
Slides across the sky on that endless root *hey*

HERACLITIS GOT IT RIGHT
(notes on the flood of '93)

We were on dry land but
the river was in the air around us,
thick & humid. As dusk blended to night,
it dampened the seats of an open windowed car.
You couldn't see it, but the river was in the cracks
& grumblings of thunder, in the dark brows
& churning stomachs of clouds; invisible,
it was in the parks & woods & marshes along the shore,
in the fields farmers plowed, in the green
life spinning out toward the sun, in the gray faces
of the boulders & the cliffs, & in the dark
caves burrowing inward.
Impalpable, the river was in the houses
that perched in its sight, it washed imperceptibly over
the proud bridges & the confident roads.
For some time now the river had withdrawn
   its attention, but it hadn't
         relinquished its claim.

It was simply inhaling, taking stock
      of itself, taking its
         time.

          *

You couldn't exactly define
the river—certainly not
as its usual channel. It was too alive
to be captured in such caricature,
too rich not to be more
complex.
        You couldn't control,
you couldn't contain, you couldn't take
for granted, no matter how hard you tried,

no matter how softly
            you let the river lull you
over the years, no matter how you sang its praise,
no matter how you hyped its land, its views,
no matter how high, how hopefully, how hard
you dammed its persistence;
no matter how you tried to sandbag
its desires.

            The river was too alive to be
unchanging; Heraclitis got it right: *you couldn't
step into the same river twice*;
                        it was bound

      to express
            its expansive nature
from time to time.

                        *

            Never argue
with a river. Better poets than I have
compared it to an ancient god. Wherever
the gods are—brother, sister—respect them.
Spit at the heavens, the proverb says,
      & you spit in your own face.
      Reflect on this,
this poet says: the same thing
happens when you spit in the river.

            *

Let us then give praise to the river.
Let us make offerings—our animals, our cars,
our homes, our lives, our various
baseball card collections. For the river came down to us
from the highest places, yea, the very heavens—
it rose up to swallow us whole.

This engulfing river tip-toeing up the steps
of the Gateway Arch to the West, this river
is all rivers. This disorderly flowing
oneness, this carrier of flotsam & waste,
this is the sacred Ganges, pouring down through
Shiva's dreaded hair, to devour, to transform,
to nourish, to shape, to revise this onflowing
poem, to curse, & to bless.

                    *

Something imperturbable about the rise of a river.
A majestic calm to meditate upon,
  (if it weren't so life threatening).

                    *

Sometimes the river flashes fiercely
& springs like a cat.

But now the river offers time,
intense geological time,
to reflect,
to consider what to do,
where to go,
what to take with you,
& what
to leave behind.

                    *

Measure
time in space
of inevitability
& inches.

The rise is slow.

Why are we here?

The river compels us to look
at the question rising
with the waters
now seeping through
our futile walls,

the boundaries between us.

What can we do?

The river compels us to look
to ourselves, to each other.

                    *

Maybe we're all drowning
in slow motion
in the thick air.

THE OTHER SIDE
for Helen Adam

Have you been to the other side?
Will you climb with me?
The other side of the mountain high
is unmapped territory

O yes I'll climb I'll climb I'll climb
I'll climb with you till the end of time
O yes I'll climb I'll climb I'll climb
I'll climb that mountain fair-o

For I've been there been there been there
O I've been there been there
The snow is falling everywhere
But I've been there been there

She takes his hand into her own
The wind is howling fierce
So cold the cold osmoses bones
As her words ring in his ears

O yes I'll climb I'll climb I'll climb
I'll climb with you till the end of time
O yes I'll climb I'll climb I'll climb
I'll climb that mountain fair-o

She draws him 'neath her red coat warm
Its fur crawls on his skin
He soon forgets the howling storm
& hears her words again

O I've been there been there been there
O I've been there been there
The snow is falling everywhere
But I've been there been there

They climb & climb & climb & climb
The snow falls blurry white
He sees flakes dancing yet feels blind
He can't tell day from night

A flash of fear: 'Go back! Go back!
You know not where you go!'
He turns around to trace their tracks
But all he sees is snow

O yes I'll climb I'll climb I'll climb
I'll climb with you till the end of time
O yes I'll climb I'll climb I'll climb
I'll climb that mountain fair-o

His legs grow leaden, fingers numb
Her fur freezes to his bones
He tries to speak—alas, he's dumb
His words come out as groans

Her hand so fastly round his own
Turns bony as a claw
It grips him tightly—then lets go!
The wind begins to roar

O I've been there been there been there—
O yes I'll climb I'll climb I'll climb—
O I've been there been there —
I'll climb with you till the end of time

The snow is swirling round & round
It spins him like a top
Around, around, around the ground
He cannot see or stop

A dancing red streak in the wood
Breaks through the relentless white
A furry tail as red as blood
His teeth flash out to bite

O I've been there been there been there
O I've been there been there
The snow is falling everywhere
But I've been there been there

An eagle soaring o'er the peak
Looks down where a timber-wolf wails
An ice-drop glistens on her beak
The wolf leaps after his own tail

O yes I'll climb I'll climb I'll climb
I'll climb with you till the end of time
O yes I'll climb I'll climb I'll climb
I'll climb that mountain fair-o

Have you been to the other side?
Will you climb with me?
The other side of the mountain high
Is unmapped territory

Unmapped territory

Unmapped territory

Unmapped territory

ANOTHER SONG FOR ORPHEUS

Orpheus' song could charm the birds, the beasts, the trees.
His verbal/vocal magic even charmed death itself
whose shadowy god permitted him
to descend to the Underworld
& bring back Eurydice, his love. Or so
Orpheus thought. We know
                the story.
Orpheus the singer returned alone.

But the point is, he returned. Back from grave Hades.
Back from the dead.
Returned the same,
but different.

If only Orpheus hadn't looked back. Had kept his living breath
on creation, on the next line
of the tale he was spinning,
on the outward unfolding
of the verse, on the burst
from the seed of unraveling stem—

If only he'd ridden that green rhythm faithfully
toward the brimming light & succeeded—
& brought back into the world, with him,
revived, renewed, his love.

But Orpheus the singer turned, & lost
the thread, found himself
in a dark sinkhole of desire
where memory was too strong. Too deeply rooted.
Love lived there. Fear
of loss.
Death.
Euryidice.

& Orpheus turned, turned
back, out of love,
dead in his tracks,
committed to memory,
marking time.

In the stillness,
Orpheus the singer
couldn't grasp the ghost—
couldn't hold love or death in that dark pit
of mind. His footing wasn't sure enough, sure enough,
in those uncertain depths.

& so, in a sense
(innocence) he fell, fell in love, fell deeper
than the most probing rooted strand,
fell ephemerally, eternally
with Eurydice
all tangled up
in the holy
grasp of death.

     *

But Orpheus returned, I said.
He returned with the spears of grass,
the bursts of weeds & flowers.
Returned the same, but different.

Orpheus returned to sing again on earth.
His strains still stirred,
the same but different (a sad refrain),
dark & jagged rhythms stirred
passions blind & grasping as human hands.
His song stirred hungers, senses
of losses & longings,
spacious & unknown
as the mind that thinks
it knows its way.

Women approached him;
drawn to his new
old, familiar song.
None were Eurydice.
Eurydice was still
far away, close
as the black hole, the pit-
falls in mind & heart.
Ecstatic,
fans sought out Orpheus, flocked round him,
desired him, & finally
overwhelmed him, & literally
took more than he had to give,
stretched him past the breaking point,
tore him apart.

Took the tatters of his clothing,
his hair, his heart, his memory
for mementos of their love, & left his limbs
beneath a tree
for beasts & birds
to gnaw; left what was left of him
for beetles & worms come up out of the earth
seeking sustenance, seeking life.

Orpheus' bones lay there
bleaching in the sun.
Men & women gathered them.
Worshipped them.
Beat them
together
cacophonously
in dim caves.

Remembering
Orpheus.

Orpheus who turned
back, but

Couldn't join
love & death.
Couldn't become his
desire.

We remember
the story.
Return to it.
Again & again & again.

It touches us
though we can't
touch it.

Looking back,
I sing of Orpheus the singer.
The same, but different.

SO LONG

fool, fool,
bent like a gnome
fool, fool,
writing the poem
fool, fool,
wants to go home

i been a fool too long too long
i been a fool too long

fool, fool,
mirror mutters
fool, fool,
student stutters
fool, fool
lover sputters

i been a fool too long too long
i been a fool too long

fool, fool,
fool day & night
fool, fool's
gold shining bright
fool, fool,
an apple says 'Bite'

i been a fool too long too long
i been a fool too long

fool, fool,
cool & calm
fool, fool,
dreaming the bomb
fool, fool,
meaning no harm

i been a fool too long too long
i been a fool too long

fool, fool,
a look in the eye
fool, fool,
born to die
fool, fool,
wondering why

i been a fool too long too long
i been a fool too long

A POET WHO DIED YOUNG
for Arthur Brown (1947-1982)

he knew the song the goldfish sang
in his window world, the slow ripple
of a lover, the sad, triumphant music
of the caged bird

   he knew & reached through
the window, the world, the cage
of the body, writing
a bop kaballah on the empty notebook pages

writing out of junebug flashings,
noting the differences between cement & concrete,
growling out belly blown improvisations
terrablue afternoons,
blowing the logic of the gone
Buddy Bolden's trumpet, the preacher's
clean scat, Mr. Parker's precise needling

      —What could language do
        to cut through
          itself—
           ?

He knew his job was to poet:
the words spoke through him, from all over
through time too, when he was really there, ready,
in the flow, when the words were heady &
moist in the corners of his mouth—

then it was *nothing but love*
nothing but love—

& he knew then
he was immortal & that he was destined
to die
      with a lopsided smile like Michaelangelo
         on his scaffold

& he thought
  death might not be
            all that bad

  except for the living

STRANGE DAYS

Strange days of March between Winter & Spring.
A death. A burial. White gloved black Masons
intone ancient ritual over black man in white coffin.
Unending prayer trails off as top-hatted leader still talking & walking. . .
leads his troops away. Walking & talking. Life trails away. . .
Prayers answer prayers like echoes
in the dim chapel light.
We're alone with our dying.

*

Worms &
grandchildren among the remains.
Tiny crocus buds
signaling in the garden. Icy puddles
in the graveyard we're walking through.
Watch your step.
Bow your head before the etched name.
Place a stone.

I was here.

CAN'T HOLD ON

All I've ever said
All I've ever done
All I've ever wanted

gone   gone

All I've ever had
All I've ever won
All I've ever needed

gone   gone

Gone like breath the changing wind
Bone to dust where once was skin
Won't ever be the same again

gone   gone
can't hold on

Gone are all the selves I've been
Gone are those who once were kin
Gone like breath the changing wind

gone   gone
can't hold on

(gate gate paragate
parasamgate bodhi svaha!)

If you're proud
Catch a cloud

gone   gone
can't hold on

If you're a giver
Bring me a river

gone   gone
can't hold on

If you dare
capture the air

gone   gone
can't hold on

If you'd be higher
Hold on to fire

gone   gone
can't hold on

At your birth
Root in the earth

gone   gone
can't hold on

(gate paragate
parasamgate bodhi svaha!)

All the dues I've ever paid
All the music that I've played
All the love I've ever made

gone   gone
can't hold on

Gone are all the selves I've been
Gone like breath the changing wind
Won't ever be the same again

gone gone
can't hold on

      gone

dan de lion

you used to stand so straight
so bright & light just like the sun

now so soon yr stooped & pooped
all frail & gray

& gone
to seed

FOOL POEM # 1
for poets

   Here we go with another
session
   pounding keys as if
to re-shape them to fit
   supple locks, & open

stubborn doors.
   O god!
the futility & the vanity
   of such an effort at dis-
covery!

   Tripping
over one's own shadow
   trying to pound
     even from sound
the stone's blood.

   Always the image
    of the Fool dances by,
some cuddly hellhound yapping
   at his heels,
        the canyon

yawning

IF NOT YOU, WHO?

You who are abandoned, you who have disappeared,
You who exist only in the resurrected photographs,
    in the statues of memory,
        the fluttering beats of lonely hearts,
You who have vanished into your own drab cells, the warehouses
of clipboards, the pinstripe prisons,
You whose parting gestures are iconic, whose words
expand like projective verse,
You who are swallowed by a jungle, declared irretrievable,
missing in action, done & gone,
You who are the final term in the equation of emptiness
that longs for a proof,
You who are erased from the blackboard of space,
You who sit calmly between whirling electrons
    who breakdown like a sugarcube in a cup of coffee
You who sparkle in a child's eye, or droop in a teardrop

You who these words surround, close in on,
You who in absence are more than a presence,
You who are vacant, obscure, wary, weary,
    who enact rituals in the morning mirrors of imagination,
You who go about your life even in death,
or your death oddly in life,
You who are lost who we cannot lose,
You who lose so we cannot win,
You who are despised, you who are idolized,
You who linger mysteriously in the air
    with your inimitable music,
You who we cannot grasp,
You who come home to our embrace,
You who span the poem's breadth,
    who breathe the poem's breath
You who we don't know, yet know,
    with every inhalation & exhalation,
    we desire, yes, we write for you whose name is

POETRY IS

motion
    poetry is
e-motion
    poetry is
he-motion
    poetry is
her-motion
    poetry is
hurt-motion
    poetry is
heart-motion

    poetry as
a notion
    poetry was
an ocean
    poetry is
come-motion

    poetry is

WORD SWORD

```
        w
        o
        r
        d
w o r d s w o r d s w o r d s w o r d s w o r d
        w
        o
        r
        d
```

MANGIA ITALIANO W/ STEVE
for Steven Pitters

south side cheap pasta eats
at mangia italiano waiting for the open mike performance bards
to begin their rites—home made noodles & healthy sauces,
salads, all you can eat, less than five bucks, a good deal
meal; restless energy of highschoolers on up
rollicking in the narrow aisles.
From my table through the front glass window I see
two teens lighting a joint; nerdy kids
burst through the aisles to hug & shriek at one another,
restless, sexual, a simulated high
to be *not* alone,
in not out—the first
poem's about a cop killer—"he did it, didn't give a shit"—
the twenty something poet is pushing it, screaming over the mike,
but no one's listening
too hard, some
not at all—
that poetry might be
the shove of personality; a slightly ill
control of the technological, not technical control
of the illogical; amplification not implication; instead of
an imposing electric voice
a voice imposing itself by electrically enhanced
volume, i.e., in my face—hadn't counted on
that direction—
the poet booms on, a poem
for "the homeless", for "love", for or against
the "suits" & "robots" swiveling in big chairs
in antiseptic offices; the particular
unseen—the reality

cops walk in, anonymously alerted, two,
a man & woman, crisply uniformed, each
only a few years older than the highschooler heads

they recoil, walkie-talkies blaring
not unlike the unheard poetry, but the cop
poem's over, the dope's already copped, the back room's empty
& in the sudden hush
                              no one knows nothing—& I say

X generation misfits, yuppie dropouts, big booming babies,
afficionados
of some mediated get-a-life nostalgic sixties never-lived,
some cool jeans commercial,
turn off
the tv in your brains—put out your own antennae—

                    write about clinking coffee cups
& *cops silencing poets*—

the best line of the night's
from a musician playing/saying

"free music, the only music
that's worth it"

CHILI-MAC
    for Allen Ginsberg

Poets want Irv's Good Food
not because of the sight rhyme
but because this is a real diner, white tiled exterior
& spinning counter stools—
the last of a dying breed in South St. Louis.
Greasy menus, Nehru capped cook, lone gray waitress,
derelicts mingling with investment brokers—
all bow & nod
to its egalitarian fare.

A genuine place. Bus stop waiters
get invited in out of the cold.
Everyone knows everyone—if you're new
you're soon named.
Ginsberg
came in & tried the Chili-Mac Special,
grilled the cook about how to make it, for who
& why. Is it popular? The interrogation
went on & on—social
research.
It all boiled down
to three words.

Cheap and filling.

Allen looked at me.

More for less, I said.
Like good poetry, he smiled.

We ordered some & it filled the bill.
More American than apple pie.
Yankee Doodle's Italian pasta,
the feather in his cap,

tickling Native American beans & peppers.
Multi-cultural dialogue afloat
in the gastric juices.
Irv asked, *Is it good?*

It was a good year
before I needed to go back.
Allen long gone from Burroughs' hometown.
I walked in the door & was greeted like a regular.

"Howyadoin' Bud?" said the chef.
"Well, well, well, Mr. Budget," chimed in the waitress.

"Where's Mac?" the chef asked.
I looked at him weird.
"You know, your friend with the beard," he said.
"Chili-Mac."

CLOSING DOWN THE BARS
for George Barlow

"I thought this was a town you could have some fun in."
Everywhere we go the bars close down.
"I thought San Francisco was an open city."
The quality of light, the twinkle in the eye of the bay
the kamikaze cocktails & the hills, graffiti on the walls
all whispered that here was where the continent went over the
brink—that here was a city built for bards.
Yet here we are, closing down the bars.
Not enough time for a guy to stare into his drink;
they're stacking tables on the chairs, waving &
shaking sorry heads though locked glass doors,
closing down the bars.
No time to return to that place where catty-cornered
ladies of the night (we finally decide) really did give us
their eyes; no time to finish out that line
of questionable reason, savor that drink
down to the dregs, write out that poem
flashed & vanished in the warm glow.
They're closing down the bars, & leaving
us to roam the hungry streets, to look out
over City Lights, to try to find the car.

I think those Chinese poets had it right.
A jug of wine deeper than thirst,
some woods, a shack, a stable or a cave
where clocks & locks don't rule;
where a glance across a smoky room won't stop your heart;
where a man can piss on his foot, get crazy
in his cups & stagger around shouting out
the shards of his broken brain to the moon;
where he can sing his off-key song to pulsing stars,
discuss desire with the universe;
where all the doors are open, or don't exist,
& the only glassy things that will close

are his eyes
when he's so blind that death looks kind
                as a sunrise, & life
laughs with the crazy crowing cocks

AT TAGORE'S DEATHBED

Navigating the rush-hour crowds of Calcutta,
the din of horns & hawkers, the excavated streets
thick with puddles of rubble, cows & their droppings,
beggars hunched on sidewalk squares, & workers wending home;
hopped a bus & stood in its stifling heat, hanging on
for dear life as it jerked & pulled & willed its way
along, through the resistant, impossible city
of your birth, Tagore; leaped off, then walked some more.
Dr. Datta, thin Virgil, beside me, talking non-stop,
serenely, all the way, of you, beloved bard of Bengal,
whose *songs still sing*, & keep you alive in this state,
this infernal, vibrant metropolis, your city, your
world—Datta knew you at *Shantihniketan*, Peace House,
your ashram school in the countryside, whose only walls
were sky, whose chalk was moon & sun, & blackboard night &
monsoon clouds; & like a Bengali, he loved you dearly.
We looked at the photos in the gallery of your family home,
now a seedy arts college, in the space where starry nights your
musical dance-dreams were first performed—youthful
you as Valmiki,
outlaw turned poet; you with politicians, philosophers,
writers—in China, London, Iraq; you prematurely
patriarchal; you with your wife, who died
halfway through your years; you with Einstein,
you with the man-miracle you named
Mahatma—you with your white Whitmanic beard flowing
over the planet, everywhere & nowhere, formless & familiar
as your *Brahmo* god—Valmiki, you wrote,
was moved by the singing & suffering of the hunted,
haunted birds to abandon banditry & become a bard;
& Walt, your American uncle, & my you, too
became a poet
out of the cradle endlessly rocking, responding
to a solitary winged singer
trilling freely, feelingly

for his departed mate. Datta says
this tragic sense
is what makes the poet.
This, no
doubt, & . . .
                    words.

We wound up at your deathbed, Tagore,
as the lights were being turned out
all around us; finally, in the dusk,
Datta & I shared a silent moment
with you—

                    then a flock of birds, black
kites, burst against the sky, with cries
raucus as downtown Calcutta, & one
settled on the sill, peered in curiously,
intelligently, I thought, & then
flew off, into the emptiness
                              to sing,
to sing, I imagined,
                    like you, Tagore,
as Datta smiled, & my solitary heart
fluttered

FAME

The Qutab tower, 'the symbol of Delhi," Mr. Joshi says,
stands brazenly, 70 metres high, marking
Islam's conquest, & immortalizing the ruler who built it—
whose name I forget.
Built it on the site, literally on top of Hindu temples:
smashed the trunks off the faces of the elephant god, Ganesha;
smashed the smiles & breasts of the *yakshi* women
clinging to its base;
no idols for this prudent dude,
just a stony erection.

& across the way, his successor tried to outdo him,
build a higher tower, get remembered longer.
But "man proposes, God disposes," Mr. Joshi says.
What you see is a squat, stubby mockery of the first.
Story is this *moghulish macher* went out one day
to admire the progress of his tower tomb.
A workman perched above, perhaps made jittery
by the static of vibrations
beaming from below, dropped a brick
momentum-usly down
upon his august presence,

nailed the *wazir*
upside the head—
& crushed him in his tracks.

They buried the deceased modestly.

No one bothered to finish the tower.

POEM FOR A PALM LEAF PAINTER

We met on the steps
of Konarak's Temple of the Sun
in the jungly lushness of Orissa.

After I followed you with my mind
you followed me with your feet.
        Got around

to showing me your wares.
        We bargained hard,
struck a deal for your palm leaf painting of Ganesha,

Shiva's son, elephant-headed boy-god,
        overcomer of obstacles,
surrounded by circles bearing Vishnu's incarnations:

a fish, a turtle, a wild boar, a dwarf,
Rama with an axe, King Rama
with a bow, flute-tooting Krishna, Buddha

beneath umbrella, jug-eyed Jugger Naut, (Jag Nath)—
you named them all—including Kalki, a riderless horse
with flaming candle burning on its back,

transformer of energies,
the avatar to come.

We talked beneath the elevated statue of the evening sun—
hundreds of feet above us
on the pyramidic steps—

serene & bronzed, dusky Surya looked
perhaps a little weary; below the sun god,
& above us, gigantic erotic sculptures:

couples coupling,
cunnilingaling—athletic, acrobatic,
voluptuous, sublime.

Your flowing black hair, painted forehead, dark eyes,
wild smile, reminded me of jazz musicians I've known
& blown with, dear friends on the other side

of the planet, home.
It was important to you that I understood
you weren't just some hustling hack, that you read

the *Gita* every day, learned the stories
behind the images, chanted the mantras,
tapped the *shakti* force to feed your art & soul.

Not the greatest artist, you admitted, but sincere.
You told me with hands & words you played flute
like Lord Krishna, knew time

on tabla & mrindangum like the *Nataraj*
god dancing life, even blew an unimaginable sax
(I could hear it as some otherworldly Bird).

Underneath your painting's incarnations
on their worlds of palm-leaf flaps—
line drawings, humans, underlying

their deific covers—
men & women making love, like
the stony figures lording over us,

kama sutra poses,
beneath the images of gods.
        Beneath the ledges, art,

                    you shrug,
& smile, hands up, to signify . . .
nothing. . . a trifle . . . a gesture

tripping
        in me

                "something
out of nothing: an exchange
                of energy," thinking, "mind

& matter, spirit & body,
        will & act,
                inspiration & realization—"

really wailing now, your hands
                & halting words provoking
                this racing mental babble.

        "Exhuberance is Beauty," I exclaim,
quoting Blake, this poet's guru,
        out of Western left field.

"Play of God," you reply,
        not missing a beat, *Shiva-shakti*,"
"om mani padme hum" (the jewel is in the lotus)

these wild rhapsodic outbursts
dissolve
to silent waves

 sound
        heat
                light

radiant, pregnant, words
floating in the air

over the language
barrier, across the cultural
gap—

playful
attraction

fills the mysterious
emptiness

sculpts the space
about us—

shapes the paint on palm leaf
held in palm of hand—

our eyes dance

& suddenly, in the wide
silence, connecting

inside & out
above & below

we meet,

a single mind,
on stony ancient steps,
before we part

FIGURES

1 plus 1
is sum
X
1

1 plus 1
is
even
2

it's odd
that
3
can be

1
2

JIM AIGOE'S SATORI

Cottonwood trees

Wind

Shhhhh

BROWN RICE

i love

making
brown rice
in the big
old pot

it will
nourish
every
body

after all
it costs
next to
nothing

to serve

THE ANTS
for Arthur Sze

At Tsankawe ruins we climb ladders
to the mesa top & look over the desolate
Pajarito Valley. Rio Grande Anasazi lived here,
the "Old Ones" who farmed the desert valleys
before America was claimed & named.
No sign of that activity now, hawks hovering overhead
the only ones working the visible earth for food.
Those who inexplicably vanished left footprints
etched deep in the cliff. We walk in these—*turistas*—
contemplating in silence this vast emptiness,
our own loneliness, as the wind rises and the profane sun
goes down.

> *When the world was destroyed by flood*
> *those humans who still could see*
> *through the door that opened at the top of their heads*
> *went down into the earth to wait.*
> *There the ant people took care of them.*
> *When the waters receded, a new world appeared,*
> *the fourth, and they emerged out of its depths*
> *to try again to live in it in harmony.*

These kivas at our feet, round brick wombs
built in the earth & now filled in with it,
represented this past to the Anasazi, reminded them
of their destruction, their emergence & rebirth.
Here they taught secrets & performed ceremonies.
Where did they disappear to, we wonder,
standing where they stood, now,
not far from the "atomic proving ground." Before us,
an anthill swells over the lip of the kiva,
& the ants scurry purposefully about,
organizing their space,
ignoring us,

& a spectacular sunset

NEW YORK CITY

traffic jamming at

Columbus Circle—gray birds

fly south in silence

THE SAINT & THE MISSION

In the great courtyard of the San Juan Bautista Mission
flowers still grow, along with scented herbs;
bees still buzz their flight patterned language,
dipping into bright petaled cushions
to sit in meditative silence, sipping honeyed bliss;
the birds still soar & flap, singing songs of longing
beneath the vast & soothing sky still a gleaming
blue; the hills still spread & ripple in all directions
shaping this verdant valley, cupping this serene & holy spot
like prayerful hands, opening, gathering clear water
for unseen lips.
In this valley, on these pathways, through this courtyard
Fray Junipero Serra walked 200 years ago, walked from the chapel
to the music room & stopped to listen to the sounds
as he sat on these stone garden benches, drinking in
the ubiquitous beauty with all his open senses.

The kiss of the Sun for Pardon
The Song of the Birds for Mirth
One is nearer God's heart in a Garden
Than anywhere else on Earth

reads a sign for the tourists who walk these paths
in increasing numbers now
that Fray Serra has been named a saint.

I wander these intoxicating garden grounds
in the warm sun, hearing no birds,
lost in my head & time,
wondering what Fray Serra prayed for.
Did he pray for the success of this & the other outposts
he established up & down California's rugged coast?
for the monks & the drunks that they sheltered? Did he
pray for the souls of "my"
mission Indians

who worked the surrounding fields & fed this holy flock?
Did he show his "red heathens" open Christian love?
or Inquisitive close-minded severity? Or a measure of each?

Did Fray Serra pray for forgiveness here in the garden,
in front of these bright multi-colored flowers?
Or later, alone, in front of a statue, in his dark chapel?
Did he pray for each of the four
thousand three hundred red souls
who resisted slavery & salvation?

Four thousand three hundred
red souls battered & murdered on these grounds,
broken bodies buried in a mass grave
beneath the serene surface,
under the dirt floor
of a barren corner room
where no plaques offer poems, no windows let in light.

Did the saint turn the other cheek
to the sight of their suffering
or, drawing the bow across his cello, nod,
& consign them to the pit?
What voice spoke to him, spoke through him in this garden?

A Vatican spokesman
denied the floggings, the forced labor,
the massacre: "No one
is beatified if there is a shadow
of a doubt about his virtue."

But there are only shadows in the empty corner room, swirling
shadows where boarded windows allow little light,
shadows blanketing the bare dirt floor, over the mass
grave at the San Juan Bautista Mission.

FOR JOETTA WHITESIDE (1952-1992)

Joetta, I have no answers.
Tears flow easier than words.
I remember how we all laughed together last
Thanksgiving, & how good it felt
responding to your needling twinkle,
your bright soul shining through the play
of light reflecting on your eyeglasses.

That memory,
that same look
in the page one photo
in Friday's paper
all we have now.
You, under glass,
under ground.

Who could, who would want to
live
in a world of Acme Avenues,
where you can be shot dead
for nothing,
in your living room,
through the feeble walls of your home?

& who could say
you are "better off dead"?
though if any of us are
with God, it would be you, now; we
are left
the worse off by your absence.
Two words the reporters used for the neighborhood: "War
Zone." Too easy
words. The morning after, the street was eerily silent, dazed,
picking up the pieces.
The snakes gone, under their rocks, the neighbors peering at nothing.

Two words they used to describe you (more
accurately): 'hardworking' and 'kind'.

I looked at your blood on the living room floor in sickening pools,
the holes the AK-47 bullets left in your walls,
Kenny standing there, shaking to my touch, staring blankly,
smoke curling up from the cigarette forgotten
wedged between the fingers at his side.
Returned from work at 3 AM,
everything gone
down.
        Masked gunmen, they said,
shooting at someone else, spraying forty rounds at least
into four buildings, two cars, two other bodies,
creasing the buttocks of your four year old angel, Kahlia.
Who would want to live in a world where a child has to watch
her hardworking and kind mother gunned down
        on the living room sofa,
gunned down by killers very likely
children themselves,
behind their masks, beyond the paper-thin walls?

You are the sacrifice
in this rite of sick manhood, where the rifles bark
out of control, & Nike'd feet
whisper incoherently through alleys of despair.

You are the sacrifice staining poverty's altar:
in the inner sanctum where no one knows
you, sweatshirt hooded monks bray
to the god of money, bow to the god of dope,
& prostrate themselves to the god of power
exploding at their fingertips.

You are the sacrifice laid low for someone's high,
someone's fear, someone's buck & boast. None
of your executioners cared

to know you. None even saw you. Who could live
in a world so blindly senseless, so aimless, so unkind?

Joetta I have no answers.
The words all come out as questions.
Two days later, a half a mile away, a thirteen year old boy
stabbed an eighty-eight year old woman to death.
What have we come to in what we call 'civilization'?
What do we tell your son & your daughter?

"Bang! Bang! Bang! Bang!"
go the little kids a few houses down
as we pray in the street, circled before your riddled door.
That's all they know, says Adelia, weeping.

How do we kill the anger, the pain, the hope-
lessness? *Bang! Bang! Bang! Bang!*
Goddammit!
The prayer turns to a curse.

Let it go.

Join the circle.
We
are the city.
This poem
is a brick.
Pick it up.
You can

throw it—

or build.

THEM

I am an endangered species
yet I am human
& I am free
living in eternity

but also from birth
on this planet earth
in the system
of Them

Them been here
since the beginning of fear
Them dragged me wailing from the womb
Them'll bury me silent in the tomb

Them granted curiosity
& planted a forbidden tree
Them's tricky, full of mystery
Them writes the book of history

Them is nameless, Them is free
Shameless as authority
Them's blameless in non-entity
The same whatever century

Them calls me woman, calls me man
Them tells me what I can't & can
Them calls me *nigger,* calls me *jew*
Them's neat as a nazi, twisted as a screw

Them etches furrows in my head
& drives me from my marriage bed
to walk the furrowed path Them paved
lonely, weary, to the grave

Them draws me close
then rends me apart
Them aches my head
Them breaks my heart

Them makes me work
& sweat & sigh
Them brings me down
Them gets me high

Them pits me against
my sister & brother
(not to mention
my earthen mother)

Them runs amok
Them calls for order
Them signs the deed
Them lines the border

Them is rich
so I stay poor
Them says 'love'
when Them means 'war'

Them is the enemy
of all mankind
Them hides somewhere
in my mind

Them smashes the atom
The end is near
Soon Them or Us
must disappear

POET'S RAP

Gather up & gather round
a poet's rap
is going down
ain't nothing new
the evening news
colorfully true
st. louis blues
aching thru
myth/history
& snaking round
the mystery
& shaking apples
from your tree
to lift you from
your gravity

> *Poet's Rap*
> *It's a killer*
> *Poet's Rap*
> *It's a killer*

Now
times are hard
careening fast
& each new day
could be our last
more reason to
use heads & hearts
& not abuse
our natural smarts
cause any answer
we can find
delving deep

in heart of mind
down in its depths
& still as stone
we understand
we're not alone

Poet's Rap
It's a thriller
Poet's Rap
It's a thriller

yet in our time
we separate
& seeds get sown
of fear & hate
this rap reminds us
real-ize
          life's unity
that underlies
our lonely separate
transient me's—
our individualities—
          & know
compassion's
what we need
to full-fill life
not self-ish greed

Poet's Rap
it's a yearning
Poet's Rap
It's life-affirming

Beau Jesus says so
Buddha too
& Martin, Malcolm
& Lao Tzu
& every animal
through whose eyes
a soul cries out
we recognize
each still small voice
says, to be free
we must express
our unity
& bathe each self
in selfless bliss
as lovers do
inside a kiss

Poet's Rap
Thou art That
Poet's Rap
Thou art That

so expand that
I-dentity
& understand
"I'm" not just "me"
& that the inside
& the out
is what we're finally
all
about
The universe is
where we are
eternity's
more near than far
the final Word is

All is One
So now you know
The rap's undone

 Poet's Rap
 It'll haunt ya
 Poet's Rap
 It's a mantra

it's a mantra

it's a mantra

CHIMAYO

at El Santuario de Chimayo,
in the mountains
north of Albuquerque—a serene garden:
butterflies airdance
round courtyard crucifixes,
tranquility here

a caged marble virgin,
love notes & offerings
stuffed between the bars,
flowers & bees
buzzing in the high grass;

in God's light, inside

El Santuario's chapel, before a
purple/white/green/& red
circus-striped altar,
a drained, beaten, skinny, wooden
     Jesus
        slumps,
   bleeding
on an aqua cross;

a threadbare
holiness
blinks in the darkness—a white candle's
flame—a weeping woman prays
on her knees in the shadows

     *

in a back room, a dirt floor, a hole
full of nothing, nothing
but its own earth, earth held
    sacred—
        believers,

from miles around, make pilgrimage here,
dip into *"el posto,"*
to gather & touch its
red clay to their pain

—Joseph Rodriguez,
21 & single, made a "personal promise to Christ" & left
El Rosado Church in Santa Fe on June 27th at 6:40 A.M.

w/his cross on his shoulders,

walked up the mountain
& passed through El Santuario's gates
at 10:45 on June 29th
the Feast Day of Peter & Paul—

his crudely
spelled testimony,
hand lettered in pencil,
one among many, nailed up with Jesus's
face, yellowing
on adobe walls
looking down on *el posto*—
the dark
woman knows
these tales of the dust
that purifies & heals

her bare feet stomp
ten times in *el posto;*

she bends,
& probes the cool earth
with her fingers—
rubs a thumb of clay
between her sunless eyes

        *

now back in the cathedral
on her knees again,
but no longer weeping
before Christ's bloody tears;

his head bowed before hers,
his suffering
(ours); our godhead
slumped—

she raises
her head, lips part to
a mystery, silent & moist

            *

earth-smudged forehead
blurry third eye
seeing everything
seeing nothing—

flicker of
candle—

all this suffering
with its circus backdrop

all this suffering

holy hole
charged with power

mysteriously illumined
in the dimmest of backrooms

mysteriously illumined
by a glistening teardrop

all this suffering

mysteriously illumined
by sunlight & flowers .

all this suffering

mysteriously illumined
by the industry of bees

& the transformation of butterflies
before us in the air—

in the garden
at El Santuario—

I am a witness, this
is my testimony, I too
touch the earth, I too
leave
this crudely lettered
love note
between the bars,
in the cage,
at the feet of
the holy mother

LOGGING COUNTRY

At the Bluebird Cafe
  the coffee cups are clacking &
everybody's talking bout the accident
yesterday on 101, one of
those big tractor-trailers
overturned,

"held up Ed for an hour."

"That's the best-behaved group of rubbernecks
I ever worked with."

   The battered baseball cap
  bobbing up & down—
      the gray trucker's
      beating gums weighing
                  relative
        highway bloodstains

on the next stool,
            young Tom, jobless at 9:40, looks
disheveled & beat—muddled
as Edna the cook
                  leans through her window
from the kitchen, & hisses
            a stage whispery steam
                        towards his ear—

     from the grill
          to the grilling—

     Tom shakes
     his sorry head,
                  his cigarette ash,
        the jar of sugar—

we order eggs "over-easy"
from name-pinned Claudette, wiseapple
waitress, shot through
the empty picture frame
to the receded Edna, Claudette commanding
"over easy Bluebird style—
with a run in it—"

"yeah," Edna crackles back
over frying bacon,
to no one in particular,
"we give it to you fast—
the way it is."

"Management Policy"
streaked with grease, hung over
Tom's counter-cradled head:

"This is *not* Burger King.
We don't do it your way.
We do it *our* way."

Strangely,
before coffee is even served,
the morning clarifies

AFTER VALLEJO

Idle on a stone, unemployed,
he looks into the river. . . Narcissus
of scrounge, fop of scruff, suit shiny
at elbow & butt, what creature stares up,
wizened & tight-lipped, out of the deep?
Having devoured the short ends of cigarettes
& the smoke of the soul, having walked through
the classifieds "Full of Jobs,"
says the President, "full of. . ."
having stood in the lines of the jobless multitudes
having filled out the forms full of the routine questions
requiring routines for answers—Who *are* you?—Who are *you*?
A man whose newspaper covers his head in the rain
who traces the lines of his face in the river
lines written by this tragic poetry
A man who stoops over in a phone booth's privacy
to count his change & cough
who haunts the harsh streets, the hiring hall warehouses
the coffee shops of oblivion
Idle on a stone, unemployed
Home is no longer home as I is no longer I
Who will offer the rag he needs to mop his brow?
Who will fill the cavity that aches his spirit?

What will the river say?

And what are
his Qualifications?
Three million years spent
developing an opposable thumb, an upright posture
A couple of million thinking, abstracting
Hundreds of thousands travelling, learning, adapting
to arrive precisely here
(Only a few thousand learning to write—
Don't hold it against him

He can dig ditches, push paper, erect pyramids
He has invented sources of light, a certain style,
a simple mirror).

He can figure things out.

Where will he go?
What will he do?
How will he fill out
his application? Can he
sign in under 'Last Job'
that he "helped a guy"?
Will he beg? Will he steal?
Or will he stay still, by the flowing river
idle on a stone, unemployed?

PISSING IN THE GUTTER
(a poem full of ugly words in praise of Beauty)

We would interrupt the game of "Johnny Fuck!"
to piss in the gutter. Watching the streams of urine
fountaining in beautiful arcs and washing the filth
gathered along the curb downhill toward the sewer.
Johnny Fuck was a simple game, a variation on tag
adapted to the four box wide sidewalk—the two outer
regions represented "shore," the two inner ones the "river"
territory of Johnny Fuck—players would chant
"Johnny Fuck! Johnny Fuck! may I cross your river?"
& "Fuck" would reply, *"not unless you wear the color ___!"*
(& he'd name his pleasure, the price of permission).
Those who could show the designated hue on their public outer
or private innerwear, could float across free,
those who didn't had to negotiate his patrol,
trying to elude JF's Loch Ness Monstor tag. If touched,
          you became "It."
The best part of the game was the profane chant, the thrill of
ritually uttering the forbidden, power-charged language.
"Johnny Fuck! Johnny Fuck!" Sounding it still
gives me perverse pleasure:

Beseeching chant, ugly as sin, I, too, proudly projected
to appease the Lord of the River.

And the forbidden act of pissing in the gutter
naturally accompanied this artless pastime, relieving
its boring repetition, its unique tension,
with release. Toeing our concrete shoreline,
River of Fuck to our rear,
ocean of gutter before us, our penises bared to the summer
air, the exhaust of blind sloopy traffic on Seaman Avenue,
touching ourselves
with the vision of a self-generated—
beauty!—from all that

was designated dirty & ugly.
Bubbles bursting in the curbside stream.
Flowing downhill.

A yellow river for Johnny Fuck.

BAMBOO
for Jomo

We sit on the curb under the highway overpass
like three old winos, watching the rain pour down,
drinking beer, enjoying
the cool breeze—Uncle Dan advising young Jomo
on the craziness of the world, corrupt city politics,
smoking & drinking—("don't wind up like me")—
the rain pounds down, floods & rushes through the gutters.
Dan invites Jomo to go to the track with him the next day,
describes the people there with their prodding probing fingers
demanding cigarettes, money, contact:
"You should go once & you should go with me. . ."
He tells Jomo about the value of friends,
about the times he had no place, but always had
a friend's home to crash: how "the only thing your dad has
that I don't is you. . . & that's a lot. . ."
The words come out in a torrent—
tells him how much he loves him, how
if anything happened to him, how much it would hurt

Jomo listens, drinks it all in: the evening suddenly cooled
the ozonish blanket of thick heat finally blown away
the baseball game long over, the bars, blues,
2 am gutter reveries
in the wind—
renewing, cleansing, driving
rain—memory
seeds already stirring. . .
the movement from childhood to adulthood before us
in these sheltered moments, under the overpass,
avuncular, toothless Danny,
me as square pops,
Jomo . . .

I watch my son,
I am without words; they are unnecessary.
He is like a shoot of bamboo creaking in the forest

GRANDFATHERS

One chain-smoked cigarettes,
rolled his own
with slow deliberate movements,
never wanted matches,
lit each new smoke
with the butt of the last.

Worked as caretaker
for a club of rich French
& German businessmen
in Salonika,
by the Aegean Sea,
where he watched
the Greeks & Turks unite
to drive out the Bulgarians.
They'd shoot at
the Bulgarians,
driving them back,
street by street.
Then they'd shoot at
each other.

Like most who lived there,
this grandfather
didn't give a damn
who won, when the smoke
cleared.
But the Germans,
the Germans cared,
& so they tried out their bombers
over the city, warming up
for 'The Great War.'

The city smoked
with this grandfather.
But each work day
ended the same way for him.
He'd sweep up his own butts,
throw them away in the trash
& consign the pile to flames.

He was a disgrace
to the family,
for he worked on the Sabbath.

His grandfather
had been head rabbi
in Palestine,
& his brother
was a rabbi in Salonika,
& a money-changer
on the side—
working out of a little booth
on a busy corner.
My father,
who became a grandfather,
remembered it well.

This changeling brother
was thought highly of
by the family.
But my grandfather,
the black sheep, swept
& saved his money.
He left for America by steamship
with his wife & oldest son, Alberto,
to keep the boy from being drafted.

My father, the grandfather,
the orphaned son,
stayed behind with his sisters,

slept five in a bed
with uncles & cousins & aunts,
& sold needles & postcards & thread
to soldiers' outstretched hands
through barbed wire fences.

He was in Salonika
during the Great Fire of 1917.
He saw British troops,
a few blocks ahead of the blaze,
spraying buildings in the Jewish quarter
with gasoline.
They preferred to destroy the city
than to let the Germans have it.
People jumped into the harbor
to escape the conflagration.

All that smoke.

When my father came to America
he took up cigars,
& eventually opened a cigar store
on Chambers Street,
near the Immigration Bureau.
His grandfather, the chain-smoker,
died of Nazi gas,
age 101.

Smoke was everywhere.

On the other side,
my mother's father
was from Jannina,
from an ancient line of Greek Jews.
In America, this grandfather
worked in a cigarette factory
& lived in Harlem.
He is best remembered

for his big, beautiful brown eyes
& for the love he showered on his wife,
his three children,
& even on distant relatives
emerging from steerage
on fogbound Ellis Island.
He died young, coughing,
in the influenza epidemic of 1919,
two years after Salonika went up in smoke.

Heartsick, my grandmother followed him
six months later, dying
before her children's eyes
on a borrowed cot—

For years
my mother thought the "deathbed"
was a special bed
people brought in for the dying.

All those babushka'd aunts
& kimona-peddling uncles
wept at the funerals,
but none took in the children.

Somehow my mother, the grandmother,
survived, taking care
from age ten
of her two younger brothers,
not letting anyone break up the family,
shifting from foster home
to foster home
& back again
to the Hebrew Orphan Asylum.

She met my cigar-smoking father,
married, &

                just after his father (my grandfather) &
about the time his chain-
smoking grandfather died,
made him a son.

The son worked in the smoke shop,
handed over Turkish
blend Camels
to hacking chain-smokers
(old proverb of Salonika Jews,
"The camel doesn't see his own hump")
swept up their butts
as they disappeared down Broadway
in their own smoke,
didn't smoke cigarettes, cigars,
didn't think he knew
his own grandfathers;
but carried on,
                imagined them
as incense smoke curled
in the lamplight, wondered;
eventually
married, became a father
of a son; a grandfather
of grandsons in the hazy future;

                lit a candle, a joint,
                watched the smoke rise,
                linger around the ceiling;

                it vanished into thin air,
                except for what remained
                inside him

POEM FOR GRANDMA

The room was dark & full of musty furniture,
plush, velvety, worn armchairs, a velour couch
draped with the lacy yellowing doilies she embroidered,
bowls filled with sucking candies on every surface,
a sense of the grave closing in, the sun banished
for some unseen offense.
Somewhere in the Bronx, circa 1950.
The radio abuzz with guys, like my father, named Joe—
DiMaggio, McCarthy, G.I. (& only last week,
I met a Cheyenne Indian who said, "My name's Joe,
but call me Angel. Too many 'Joes' in this world,
not enough 'Angels'). She came from Ios, the island
where Homer was born, or so the story goes, as Rebecca tells it.
   She was a Romaniot,
who Grandpa had to teach Ladino.
Got out of Salonika
before the Great Fire set by the British
destroyed the Jewish quarter, before the Turkish bombings, before
World War I, before
the Holocaust, before
all her children.

From that clear Greek birthlight
to smoky steerage, Harlem, another
language (she'd teach him), another
walkup cave on another island, another
beginning to manage: brisses & weddings,
the complexities of lives
   never fully here;
   & the burial arrangements, remembering . . .
   the passage . . .
of time, each moment a gravestone
knocked over, a piece of candy offered
to sweeten the conversation,
   the accented word

exhaled into the traffic's exhaust,
a stitch in the tapestry, steady
gnarling hands
barely moving in the dimness,
slipping the needle in
& out, & later, lighting
yartzite candles, dark-eyed wrinkles
turning back, & squinting, to see
the pattern.

    Dusk
in the worn plush Bronx, alone,
toothless, still squinting

(outliving the others),
in this oppressive shade. Lucky
to be an immigrant smile slowly woven
through New York's patchwork bustle.
    A fixed jaw. A crack
    in the drawn curtains
    of the twentieth century.
A patch of light on the drab dusty rug.
An imperious, stubborn strength beaming down
on her little grandchild.
Michael

VIGIL

When I was six I bet my cousins which elevator
would go higher, faster. We stood together
before hermetically sealed doors, & rooted

for arrows gauging an ascent, swinging horizon to horizon,
we cheered gazing upward
watching numbers ticked off

as on a sped up semi-circular clock, arrows whizzing
like real time as you get older,
past the floor where our grandmother lay dying;

& on, upwards
toward the hospital's heavenly penthouse, which neither
pneumatic chariot of our racetrack imaginations

ever quite reached—
before plunging precipitously
toward the grandstand lobby where we stood, & lower

to subterranean floors, mysteries, depths.
Grandma lay dying.
We didn't know what to think, or feel, or cheer about that.

Better not even to watch, mesmerized,
on the ground floor, by a sense of the eternal
up & down motion of life

COMING TOGETHER
for Adelia

Where the Mississippi & Missouri meet
I met you, princess of the Nile.
We smiled across the table of Kansas
with its gigantic bouquet of corn.
You drew me toward you like the sea
does a river like the sun a flower
like some vast black hole in space
pulsing with contained light;
you swallowed the white night, wrapped me
in your Afric cloak, filled a bowl
with herbal smoke & pulled long & deep
& I drew too the musky draft
long & deep like the Mississippi itself
long & deep winding down from the frozen north
to southern marshy climes.
The dark willows of the south enfolded us
the balconies of New Orleans
the tomb of its voodoo queen
Marie Leaveau we stood below
its white stone face, streaked with human blood
& graffiti'd with cryptic scratches left by feline souls;

& we drew again long & deep
swallowing the night of flaming crosses
robed & hooded riders
limp bodies swinging 'neath the shadows of trees
Negress & wandering Jew
we swallowed these sad histories—
nazis, billyclubs, snarling dogs, inquisitioners,
        massahs, priests & governors
whirling in the smoky Mississippi—
enslavement in Egypt, America, the body
whirling & winding in the smoke up to the sky

104

white as the bones of the death camps
white as the tufts of cotton plants
white & whirling in the night

Your Moses came floating to you
on a raft of vegetation
buoyant with meditation
He saw himself reflected in your eye
A pharoanic sigh clouded overhead
            The spirits of the dead clucked their tongues
Out of the jungle came a rumble of drums.
A dixieland trumpet cried over the river
crumbling levi walls inside our minds
letting the river rush & wind
freely to the open sea
bearing you & me
& the burden of our history
bearing you & me
on the waves of sacred mystery

            Children of the Sun—
                    Man & Woman—

        One

(our exiles
    masked by knowing smiles

AFTER THE RAIN

robins
       hopping
             looking
                      down for worms
                & up
       for other
robins

SONNET 4-D FOR BLACK HOLE LOVE

Black Hole Sunshine, lighting dark life, kindle
These embers tickling my soul like bitter ash.
Your event horizon's too hot to handle,
Yet, drawn to your singularity, I'm cold as cash.

Black Hole Sunshine, you compress energies
Like proverbial camels passing through needles' eyes.
These together vibrations suggest synergies
Beyond anything I've up to now realized.

Black Hole Sunshine, your beams leave my vessels shattered,
Your divine sparks spill all over, yes, I've fallen for you.
& so, on my knees, here's what light I've re-gathered,
Poured into your *ginnunga gap* to shade your black blue.

(Mocking matches lit to mystery, worthless words of spaced out rhyme;
Mad meters measuring endlessness, as we ache & break thru time)

THE CREED OF THE SEED

How something so BIG
comes from something so little
A seed is the material form of need
Each of us was once a seed

A seed with a plan
to become a human
that grows & needs
& breeds its own seeds

with plans of their own
to become fully grown

need, urge
constriction, surge—
inhale, ex,
attraction, sex

seeds alight
feeling all right
taking hold
as they unfold

& so it goes, on & on
life just flows, eon to eon

all those seeds, with all their needs—
all of life just breeds & feeds

creating motley earth's
unrelenting birth

& so something so BIG
comes from something so little
& the need in the seed's
at the heart of the riddle

MOON IN PISCES

Moon in the water.
A thousand ripples.

Constantly changing faces
mirror the same face.

About the Author

Michael Castro has long been a poet and arts activist. In 2000, Castro received the "Guardian Angel of St. Louis Poetry" award from River Styx for his long service to its reading series and magazine, both of which he co-founded in 1975. Castro has given poetry readings on three continents and, over the last three decades, has collaborated in performance with a wide variety of musicians and composers. He has published six poetry chapbooks, a book of translations of contemporary Hungarian poetry, *Swimming in the Ground*, with Gábor G. Gyukics, and *Interpreting the Indian*, essays on Native American influences on Modern Poetry. Castro hosts the radio program *Poetry Beat* and teaches at Lindenwood University.

Books by Michael Castro

Ripple (with Michael Corr, Alan Fleck, and Jay Zelenka), Hard Times
          Press, 1970.
The Kokopilau Cycle, Blue Cloud Quarterly Press, 1975.
Ghost Hiways & Other Homes, Cornerstone Press, 1976
Cracks, The Cauldron Press, 1977
Interpreting the Indian: Twentieth Century Poets & the Native
          American, University of New Mexico Press, 1984;
          University of Oklahoma Press (paperback edition), 1991.
(US), Ridgeway Press, 1991
River City Rhapsody (with Eugene B. Redmond, Marcia Cann, and
          Jane Bidleman), Southern Illinois University Press, 1993.
The Man Who Looked Into Coltrane's Horn, Caliban Press,1997.
Swimming in the Ground: Contemporary Hungarian Poetry
          (co-translated by Gábor G. Gyukics), Neshui Publishing,
          2001.